ALDANTE S. BALL

BUSINESS
AND
LIFE TRANSFORMATION

Contents

Chapter 01

Introduction 1

   1.1 Working From Home: The Possible Health Benefits 2

   1.2 Working From Home: The Health Risks 4

   1.3 What You Will Learn...7

Chapter 02

Create your 'Smart' Lifestyle Design..9

   2.1 Lifestyle Design: The Alternative 10

   2.2 Digital Nomad? Or Digital Homebody 12

Chapter 03

Set-Up your Work Culture 15

   3.1 Your Work Environment 16

   3.2 Setting Up a 'Mobile Command Center' 18

   3.3 Creating Your Home Office...20

   3.4 Some Health Tips for Working at a Computer....................24

Chapter 04

Staying Discipline

Staying Discipline 28

4.1 Accepting Work...29

4.2 Choosing Clients 31

4.3 Revenue Streams 33

4.4 Targets 34

4.5 Systems 34

4.6 Hypothesis Testing 38

4.7 Your Personal Life..39

Chapter 05

Optimizing Performance, Health and Productivity 41

5.1 Optimizing Sleep...42

5.2 Exercise 43

5.3 Nutrition...45

5.4 Introducing Kaizen 47

Chapter 06

Home Business Models 49

6.1 Top Home Business Models for Lifestyle Design 50

Conclusion 54

Chapter 01

Introduction

———◆———

If you run a business from home, then it's important to recognize that it's going to mean living a completely different lifestyle from the majority of people you know. Not having a commute in the morning, not spending all day sitting in an office and being able to generally create your own working hours puts you on an entirely different page from most people you'll know.

For the most part, this is a good thing. Being able to set your working hours, to dictate the way you work and *when* you work and getting to spend time doing something you love can all contribute to a much happier and healthier lifestyle on the whole. In fact, it's a starting point for improving overall health.

At the same time though, this type of lifestyle also brings with it its own challenges. And because very few people live the same lifestyle you do, that means you're going to be somewhat 'on your own' when it comes to finding advice on how to manage this work/life balance.

Well, until you found this book anyway!

Here's the long and the short of it: being self-employed and working from home gives you the freedom to begin your own 'lifestyle design'. This is pretty much the way things are moving and is likely the future of working. Technology is making it possible for us to work remotely in more and more industries and more and more roles. The benefits of this kind of work drastically outweigh the cons – for both the employee and employer – and so the traditional office may soon become a rarity rather than the norm.

That means the emphasis is on increasingly more of us to look after our own health and work/life balance. This book will help you to do just that.

1.1 Working From Home: The Possible Health Benefits

As mentioned, when done right, working from home has the potential to lead to *incredible* health benefits.

Let's look at the facts. Most of the population is overweight, overtired and overstressed. If you can still remember working in an office, then no doubt you will recall what it felt like to have a full on day in the office, to travel home for an hour on the train/bus or in the car and then to have to cook dinner when you got back.

What did you most often end up doing? You threw something in the microwave and you collapsed in front of the television. And then when your friends called to invite you out, you ignored that and carried on 'vegging out'.

Many of us talk about 'time management' and we say that the reason we don't stick to a training regime/weight loss program is that we don't have the time. This is in fact all wrong. Most of us have plenty of *time* (otherwise, how did you manage to fit in the entire series of *Lost* recently?) but what we lack is the energy. Without energy, we don't have will-power. Without will-power, things don't get done and we start to drown in a list of things we need to be doing and become incredibly stressed. Our bodies suffer, our relationships suffer and we don't live life to the fullest.

Working from home can change all that. Working from home means that you can choose to work out in the morning or in the afternoon – you just have to choose the time that you have the most energy. At the same time, it means you can put food on the stove while you're working and watch it simmer.

Working from home means you can sit outside and feel the sun on your face, instead of being cooped up in an office (which is known to contribute to stress and depression). Working from home means that you don't have to commute down busy streets with hundreds of people walking at you during rush hour – this wreaks *havoc* with your heartrate.

In short, when you work from home you get to choose your priorities and you reduce the stress of working several times over. Now you can put yourself *first* and that's an incredibly important and valuable thing to be able to do.

The potential health benefits are transformative and life-changing. This book will show you how to start working from home if you don't already *and* how to take maximum advantage of that situation so that you're able to feel your very best and feel the benefits in every other area of your life.

Oh and of course this will have a powerful knock-on effect and impact on your productivity helping you to get more work done and to a much higher quality.

1.2 Working From Home: The Health Risks

But this book won't *just* be about capitalizing on the amazing health benefits of working from home. Just as importantly, we'll be looking at the potential health *risks* that working from home can pose. And make no mistake: there are many.

Think being shouted at by your boss is stressful? How about being shouted at by 10 angry clients? Or 300 angry customers who just downloaded your app?

And here's the difference between working for someone versus working for yourself: when you work for someone else and you have an unproductive day, you still get paid.

When you work for yourself and you have an unproductive day? You get *nothing*.

Have a bad month? You still get nothing. That's another thing: working for yourself is highly volatile and unpredictable and that's why some people refer to bipolar depression as 'the entrepreneur's disease'.

Here's another difference: when you work for yourself, none of your friends or relatives will respect the fact that you have to work during the week. 'Oh, he/she works from home, so of course they can come and help me move out of my house/meet for lunch on a Wednesday afternoon'. Never mind that you promised your clients their work would be finished at 4pm. Never mind that you'll now have to work until 5am through the night.

And on the flip side of this, your clients won't respect that your home time is your home time. They'll think nothing of e-mailing you at 5am in the morning on a Sunday to tell you the work you handed in three days ago was rubbish.

And you'll have the same problem: you'll always be tempted to finish a little early on a Friday, or to work a little late on a Wednesday. Goodbye body clock! Goodbye healthy sleep! Goodbye *good quality work*.

Then there's the fact that working from home means working on your own, with no one around, in the same room you're likely to spend your evening in. You never get to leave this space and you never get any outside interaction or input. Talk about cabin fever! Heeeeere's Johnny!

Working from home gives you freedom and that freedom can give you the option to become incredibly healthy, happy and effective. At the same time though, freedom also comes with responsibility. Fail to manage that time well and it can all go wrong…

1.3 What You Will Learn

That's the general idea and an outline of the sorts of things we'll be learning in this eBook. More specifically though, you will learn:

- What lifestyle design is and what it has to do with your health and your business
- How to apply discipline and structure when you have none
- How to avoid cabin fever
- How to manage your workflow and communicate with your clients and customers

- How to fit the right diet and training regime in around your work
- How to sleep better and see this impact on your productivity
- How to incorporate travel and spending time outside into your work
- How to work from home with your family still there
- How to transition to working for yourself
- How to generate passive income

Overall, by the end of this book you should have the tools to create a business model and an environment that allows you to maximize your health, your happiness *and* your productivity. If you already have a home business, you can use this advice to restructure your routine and setup to support a happier and healthier you.

If you don't, then you can use this book to give you the confidence and the know-how to take the leap in a way that will have the very best outcome for you.

Chapter 02

Create your 'Smart' Lifestyle Design

— ◆ —

I briefly touched on the idea of lifestyle design. What does this mean precisely?

The term 'lifestyle design' was either coined or popularized by Tim Ferriss in his book *The Four Hour Workweek*. The idea behind it is simple: you create the lifestyle you want out of your job.

This simply means that you think about the lifestyle you want and then you choose a career/build a business to support that.

For most of us, this works in the entirely opposite way. Most of us will find ourselves 'landing in a job' and from there we then see the rest of our lifestyles forming around that. We get a job and right away that dictates where we are going to live, so we normally move to that area.

At the same time, it tells us which hours we are going to work and depending on how far away we live, this will also have to include some time for a commute.

Some people will move away from their friends and family so that they can work the job they have or will even breakup relationships that were otherwise going well – all because of their jobs! And don't get it confused: these aren't jobs that they've always wanted. These aren't 'dream careers' that they have been thinking about since a young age.

No, these are jobs that they 'just kind of landed in' and are now too afraid to leave. And they're completely dictating their lives.

2.1 Lifestyle Design: The Alternative

So how does lifestyle design work in principle?

You start out by asking:

"What type of life do I want?"

And from there, you then ask: what type of job would best facilitate that lifestyle?

If you want to spend more time with family, if you want to work while travelling the world, if you want to have a career that you find fascinating and that you're proud of... then often the first step to achieving the right lifestyle will be starting to work for yourself and online/from home.

Next you have to ask whether you want to be a busy 'high flier' or whether you'd be happier as someone whose career was 'light', flexible and would largely run itself a lot of the time. This is an important point. Many people make the mistake of thinking they want to be 'really successful' in the most stereotypical of senses and as such they create business plans that involve taking on large numbers of staff with branches all over the world. The reality of being involved in this type of business though is that you now have no time to do things that contribute to a happy and healthy life. Likewise, you now are just as stressed and as tied down – if not moreso – than you would have been if you were working for a big organization in an office.

If you *want* to be a high profile businessman/woman then that's great. If not, then you need to rethink your business plan. If you want to take it even further in the *other* direction and live the most relaxed lifestyle possible, then ideally you want some kind of passive income – meaning that you generate money while you sleep. This might mean selling a digital product or it might mean hiring a manager to run the day-to-day elements of your business.

Either way, a business that 'runs itself' allows you to live the life you want and to reap the rewards for your hard work later on.

2.2 Digital Nomad? Or Digital Homebody

Perhaps one of the ultimate expressions of lifestyle design is to become a digital nomad. In fact, to many people these two terms are synonymous and interchangeable.

A digital nomad essentially is someone who works online so that they are not dependent on a physical location for their career and income. They then are free to go ahead with their lifestyle design but rather than just being content to spend more time at home, they aim bigger and travel the world.

The archetypal image of the digital nomad is someone sitting by a huge waterfall in the middle of nowhere, typing on their laptop. Or perhaps it's of someone sitting on the beach, sipping cocktails and firing off e-mails to their clients.

This is of course highly appealing for many of us and is certainly a way of living that is more 'free' than what most of us are used to. This way, you can see the world, meet new people and take each day as it comes – never knowing where you're going to end up.

That's an exciting prospect and certainly it can lead to a healthy attitude to life (and tan for that matter) for many of us. However, it also certainly is not for *everyone*.

Why? Because for starters, you'll be travelling with just a backpack and you'll never get the chance to have a proper bath and to change into fresh clothes that you washed with fabric softener. Likewise, if you're partial to a cup of tea/coffee with milk… good luck getting it.

Also, you can't have a pet dog. And for that matter, a relationship really. You'll be away from your friends and family and it will be scary. Travelling permanently can be very stressful *in itself* and you'll spend a lot of time in dodgy hostels worrying about your laptop.

But you don't have to take an 'all or nothing' approach to being a digital nomad. Instead, you can travel the world in short bursts. Or you can go on lengthy 'staycations'. Or you can just do three holidays a year instead of one.

Travelling isn't that expensive anymore. If you fly short haul then you can go to some pretty exotic places for $50 and if you are smart about when and how you buy, you can also travel a long way on the train relatively cheaply. While you're travelling, you can be working on your computer and that means you can earn some (or all) of your money back. Remember too: you can travel during the quieter times when everyone else is at work, meaning quieter resorts and lower prices.

Then, you can be working in a chalet in France, or at your friend's house in Mexico. And you can do this for four or five days, several times a year and still feel like you're getting to experience more of life than your office-bound friends. At the same time though, when you start to miss home, you can travel back and cuddle up with your wife and kids by the fire.

With smart lifestyle design, you can have your cake and eat it!

Chapter 03

Set-Up your Work Culture

———————◆———————

This following chapter is going to be aimed mainly at those who choose *not* to go the digital nomad route. Either you're someone who is content to just have more freedom working from home, or you're working from home part of the time and travelling when the opportunity presents itself.

Either way, the rest of the time you're going to need somewhere to work and you're going to need some structure. If you're already working from home, then you should read the following chapter carefully and perhaps modify some of your current routine/setup. If you're *planning* on working from home, then you should use this when creating your business model and the parameters for your productivity.

3.1 Your Work Environment

Before you can start working from home, the first thing you need to ask yourself is *where* you will actually be working. In other words, where will you be physically located as you type/answer e-mails/program.

Remember: we're focused on creating a lifestyle and a business model that will support health, happiness and productivity. *Where* you're working is a big part of this and being able to decide on the specifics of your work environment is one of the big advantages of working for yourself. So make the most of it!

Working From Home, But Not From Home

The first point to bear in mind here is that working from home doesn't have to *mean* working from home. We've already seen that when we discussed becoming a 'digital nomad'. You can take a similar approach more locally though too, by just taking a laptop out with you and working in local coffee shops or libraries.

This has a lot of advantages as compared with working from an office in your own home. For starters, when you work in a coffee shop, you get to leave the house. This is important because it psychologically separates your work life from your home life and makes it that little bit easier for you to 'switch off' when you get home. At the same time, it also means you will be taking some steps. Remember: it is recommended that we take at least 10,000 steps a day and failing to do so is bad for your heart leading to a shorter life *and* causes obesity and back problems.

Another benefit is that this way you also get to meet people. Again, this is quite an important point because spending all your time at home on your own can leave you feeling a little restless and isn't terribly healthy. By heading out to a coffee shop on the other hand, you will get to at least be *around* other people who are working and you'll get to interact with the baristas who work there.

If you want to go one step further, you can also look into a shared workspace. There are lots of these kinds of initiatives around these days and especially in larger towns. Not only do these then offer you the chance to get out of the house, but you'll also get to spend time with people who are there doing something similar to you. This creates networking opportunities and furthermore means the working environment will be entirely geared towards the kind of work you are doing. That means you'll get good wi-fi and peace and quiet as standard. Some shared workspaces even give you your own landline and PO Box.

There are other options for where you want to work too – for instance you could always head to a quiet pub or even a bar, or you could sit outside when the weather is nice. Sitting outside is of course great from a health perspective but unfortunately is somewhat lacking in terms of practicality and convenience. To do this well, you'll need to contend with glare on the screen, the lack of somewhere to sit and prop your laptop, bugs, dirt, grass and no power or wifi. Still though, perhaps there's somewhere near you that accounts for all this? Maybe you have a bar with some outside seating that's quiet during the day and faces the beach? The world is your oyster when you work 'from home'.

3.2 Setting Up a 'Mobile Command Center'

If you're going to work wherever you like though (or become a digital nomad), then you're going to need to have something to work *with*. Any small laptop will do the trick and should slip snugly into a shoulder bag or a backpack. You may be limited in terms of the operating system you can use but if not, the MacBook Airs are *particularly* light and convenient as are Chromebooks (the latter are also very affordable).

For Windows users, the Surface Pro 3 is a *fantastic* portable machine. This device is essentially a tablet with a slim keyboard built into its cover. It works on your lap (unlike some previous models) and weighs barely anything. What's more, it has beefy specs (up to i7 with 8GB), neat features (particularly the digitizer pen) and a long battery life. The 'Surface 3' (minus the 'Pro') is also very good, being a little smaller and cheaper but on an Atom processor.

If you want to be even less weighed down this was my first go to item, you can go a step further and look at one of the many 8" Windows tablets. With one of these plus a portable Bluetooth keyboard and mouse, you can do pretty much anything you would do on a small ultrabook and never feel weighted down. They tend to have 1-2GB RAM, very long batteries and retail for about $1-200. That means you can take them on a holiday and not worry *too* much about anything happening to them.

In fact, you can even *combine* a Surface Pro 3 with an 8" tablet and use it to extend your screen – now you have a multi-monitor setup even in coffee shops! It looks pretty insane and it's great for true productivity on the move.

3.3 Creating Your Home Office

On the other hand, you might decide that you *do* want to work from home. This is fine but you need to be strict about the way you're going to do it to ensure you maintain that separation between your home life and your work life and to keep yourself healthy.

The first tip then is to make sure that your home office really *is* a home office and not just a table in your living room. Oh and *never* work in your bedroom. In fact, the ideal scenario is that you *only* use your bedroom for sleeping and for sex. That way, when you head into the room your body and mind will automatically start gearing down for sleep. If you spend part of your day working in the room, then you'll find it's hard to switch off, even when you're under the covers.

For these same reasons, you want to try and choose a room to be your home office that is closed off and that is away from the rest of your property. This way, you can create that separation and it will also mean you're less likely to get disturbed when working from home while your family is there or other people are in the building. Soundproofing is obviously ideal but not necessary.

The next important thing to think about when making your home office is light. Some people actually create 'office pods' these days at the end of their garden, which are mostly-glass sheds that allow them to work as though they're surrounded by nature. You don't have to go that far but *do* try to let in lots of light and to fill the room with natural things.

Large windows (that are positioned so as not to create glare) and lots of house plants have been shown to help fight depression and stress. What's more, having a 'natural' view can also boost creativity by lowering our heartrate and allowing our minds to wander.

Another important way to maintain your health is to think about the way you'll be sitting. This means making sure that you are upright, with the small of your back well supported by a chair. You should position your monitor so that it is roughly the same height as your eyes with your chin parallel to the floor. If you are looking down all day, you'll develop rounded shoulders and kyphosis. Your hands should be hovering above your keyboard (don't let your wrists rest on the table) and you should be high enough that your elbows are comfortably at a right angle as you type.

If you want to optimize your office for maximum health benefits, then you should also consider getting a standing desk. The best standing desk designs use a collapsing frame that allows you to work either sitting down *or* standing up. It can be hard to concentrate for long periods while standing, so you might not be able to do this the whole time. However, when you are just answering e-mails or perhaps doing something with design software, standing up can give your back a real break and will help you to burn more calories at the same time.

As for the rest of your home office design, go mad and decorate it however you like. The more color, the more life and the more points of interest, the better. While you might think that sounds distracting, it actually makes your environment much 'richer' from a psychological perspective and that has been linked to triggering 'flow states' – states of intense concentration and high productivity. The more engaging your environment is, the more dopamine and adrenaline you will produce and the more focused you'll be at all times.

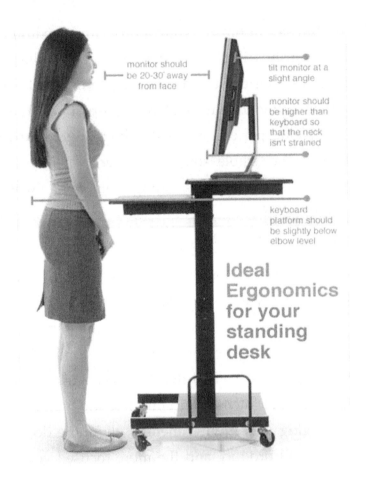

monitor should
be 20-30' away
from face

tilt monitor at a
slight angle

monitor should
be higher than
keyboard so
that the neck
isn't strained

keyboard
platform should
be slightly below
elbow level

Ideal
Ergonomics
for your
standing
desk

3.4 Some Health Tips for Working at a Computer

Regardless of whether you're working on a beach in Thailand, from a home office, or at your local coffee shop, there are a couple of health considerations you need to bear in mind which can make a big difference.

Move Regularly

Sitting correctly at the desk, or getting a standing desk can both help you to avoid some of the pitfalls of sitting at a desk all day.

Better yet though? Just move around a lot and that way you'll avoid seizing up and you'll be trying out different positions. If you have a home office, then you should invest in a comfortable chair and desk; but likewise you should also give yourself some alternative places to work whether that's a sofa or it's a beanbag in the corner of the room. Now you'll have the option of switching your position in the room whenever you become uncomfortable.

Also important is just to get up every hour or so, even if just for ten minutes. All this can help to prevent the shortening of your quads, the weakening of your hamstrings and the shortening of your pecs that lead to poor posture, back and knee pain and poor mobility. Moreover, it will help prevent the atrophy of your heart which can significantly shorten your expected lifespan.

Get a Mechanical Keyboard

If you're typing a lot on a daily basis then you open yourself up to repetitive strain injury, arthritis and other issues. A mechanical keyboard can help you to avoid these problems, by giving you something to type on that's specifically designed to be ergonomic, comfortable and supportive. A good mouse can also make a big difference.

Consider Dvorak

Dvorak is an alternative keyboard layout to Qwerty that is said to be more efficient. It essentially puts all of the most commonly used letters in the easiest to reach positions and this in turn can speed up typing while at the same time reducing the risk of arthritis.

It takes a while to learn and the research surrounding Dvorak is not concrete. Nevertheless, if the idea appeals to you then give it a go and you may find it beneficial.

Avoid the Screen at Night

If you're going to be working late into the night – which you may well do despite your best intentions – then you should consider using software to redden the screen, or maybe try wearing 'blue blocking' glasses. Unfortunately, the nature of the wavelength of light produced by most computer monitors is such that the brain mistakes it for sunlight and reacts by producing more cortisol and less melatonin. This makes it much harder for you to sleep and leaves you restful throughout the night; so use these two techniques to avoid that problem.

Protecting Your Eyes

Do you sometimes find yourself wishing you didn't have to look at a screen all the time? Does it give you a headache/make you worry about your eyesight?

Here's the good news: looking at a screen actually *isn't* bad for your eyes. Studies found that people who sat closer to the computer/TV had worse eyesight but they had the correlation the wrong way round – people sat closer to the screen *because* of their *preexisting* poor eyesight. In fact, playing computer games actually improves your visual acuity by forcing you to be aware of your surroundings.

The only danger that comes from looking at computer screens then is caused by glare and changes in brightness. It's going from a very bright screen to a dark object in the room, or going from text with glare to text without glare, that forces the eyes to work hard and readjust focus. This can wear out the muscles and *that's* when you get headaches.

So make sure that you do work to avoid glare. If you're going to be working on the go make sure your computer has a flexible hinge to avoid direct light and choose your spot carefully. If you're working from home, just make sure you have no windows or lamps in front of the screen. Keep the room you're working in light and if it *does* get darker, turn the brightness of your monitor down too. Do this and you should find you have no reason anymore to worry about your eyes while working.

Chapter 04

Staying Discipline

————————➤◆◆◆————————

If you follow all the advice in the last chapter you should now have a working environment that is conducive to good health and you should know how to avoid some of the common dangers of working from home/at the computer.

What you still need to do as well though, is think about the *psychological* aspect of your work and the way you're mentally separating one from the other.

This is where so many people who work from home go wrong. We start out with the best of intentions (set working hours, a separate work phone) but the temptation to work late one night, or to work on a Sunday, will always rear its head once we start getting behind. Problem is, this is habit forming and it creates a bad pattern. This is especially true if you work late on a weekday, as you'll then have less energy to work again on the *next* weekday and that in turn will mean you're tired and lethargic and unproductive... meaning there's a good chance you'll be tempted to work late again. As we'll see later, sleep should be considered sacred if you work from home. And for *everyone* for that matter...

What you need to do then is to set yourself strict specific parameters for working and to *not* work outside of those. This means that you have to *start* working at a very specific time and end at a very specific time. And if you run over and work looks like it's going to be late? Then you have to just accept that it's late. It's not worth ruining your life to keep a client happy – remember the whole reason we're working this way in the first place is to live the lifestyle *we want*.

Of course it's better that you *do* also keep your client happy and this is where time management comes in – as well as generally taking the right approach when managing your clients and knowing how to accept work and projects. You also need to put systems in place that will help you to manage a workflow and to become scalable even as an individual. And guess what? That's what we'll be looking at in the rest of this chapter...

4.1 Accepting Work

A big challenge as an entrepreneur or as any kind of sole trader is trying to find work. Dry spells are pretty devastating when you have bills to pay and a family telling you to 'get a real job' and if you run a service-based business, no orders means no money.

But what's *also* a really big challenge is learning to say 'no'. Learning to turn down clients, or to say 'you can have the work in a week, I'm busy right now'. We're afraid to do this because we don't want to be in that situation where we have no work but as a result, we end up taking on much more than we can chew and working insane hours that prevent us from sleeping. Worst of all, the work you hand in probably won't be as good as it could be because you'd have been rushed.

So sometimes, you have to be strict and you have to tell your client it will be a few days before you can get work to them. That's okay – in fact it's pretty much normal. As long as you tell them up-front how long it will take, you don't need to feel bad about being just one human. Do your job well and they should normally be able to wait (unless their work is time-sensitive also). If it's a web design, some SEO, an article… a couple of days likely won't make much difference to their business plan.

The same goes for turning down work that you really aren't confident with or that you really don't want to do. Just tell your client that there are others that will do a better job for less money instead of killing yourself trying to learn a whole new skill set. Be strict about what it is that you do and do that one thing very well. You'll be happier, life will be simpler and the quality of your output will be higher.

And in fact, when you tell your clients how long it's going to take, you should actually be pessimistic about it. This is called 'under promising and over delivering' and it basically means saying that things will take longer/cost more/be worse and then providing a pleasant surprise. This strategy is great from a business perspective because it gives you the opportunity to impress your client, which leads to a memorably positive interaction that will make them more likely to want to use your services again.

What's more though, under promising means that if things go wrong and you can't finish work as quickly as you probably should, you'll still have time to get your work in on time the next day. It's a simple strategy that will massively reduce the amount of stress that you find yourself under. And if you're worried you won't get as many orders this way, you can always give an 'expected completion time' and a 'promised completion time' as separate numbers.

Bear in mind that you absolutely cannot rule out the possibility of getting your work in late. There will always be times when things come up unexpectedly – at the very least it's important to remember that you won't get any paid sick leave as someone who is self-employed. (That said, you *also* mustn't be afraid to occasionally 'phone in sick' with clients as again it's more efficient in the long term).

4.2 Choosing Clients

So sometimes you need to turn down work that you get offered, or just say you're handing it in late. Other times however, you should turn down entire clients.

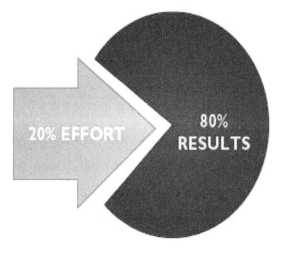

That's because there is very much a thing as a 'good client' versus a 'bad client'. Bad clients are the ones who involve too much 'communication overhead' (meaning they e-mail all the time about petty things, ultimately costing you time and money). They're also the ones who pay late (or not atall) and who are never satisfied with your work. What you'll find is that some clients fit this description, while others are polite and send the minimum number of e-mails necessary for you to work together. It's the latter kind you want to work with as it will ultimately save you a *lot* of time and stress down the line. Again, picking and choosing clients is one of the big advantages when it comes to working for yourself.

3: http://www.mattbodnar.com

Another type of client you probably want to lose, is the type who orders tiny amounts of work. The more clients you have with small orders, the more relationships you need to manage, the more projects you have to order and generally the more stressed you are likely to be. This is called 'Pareto's Law' or the '80/20' rule. The idea here is that usually it's just 20% of your customers who provide about 80% of your yields – and that you should focus on that 20% instead of the other 80.

4.3 Revenue Streams

All this said, you *do* want to try and avoid a situation where you have all of your eggs in one basket. In other words, if you turn down *all* your clients and end up with just one, then you're going to be in a bit of a sticky situation should that one client suddenly quit.

The ideal situation is to try and spread your workload between 3-4 clients. And in terms of income, you should be able to survive relatively well even if you lose *two* of those clients. The same goes if you're selling a product from your website, or if you're selling an app... have *multiple* apps and multiple products.

It's even a good idea to have an entirely separate revenue stream. Let's say you're a web designer with several big clients. As a designer you might go some lengthy patches where you don't have any work coming in and as such, you should make sure that you have a monetized website, an app or something else that is bringing in a little extra cash. You could even leave the house some days and offer your services as a fence painter by driving around the neighborhood.

In other words, you need as many revenue streams as possible, you need backup plans and you need contingencies. With all these in place, you'll be less reliant on steady work and you'll thus be less tempted to take on more work than you can manage during the busy periods.

Another tip is to use your quieter days to put work in ahead of time. For instance, if you're a web designer, you can always try designing some unique fonts or some website templates that you can use later on to save yourself time. This way you'll be able to take on more work later on, without feeling overwhelmed.

4.4 Targets

While managing all this work, it can be useful to set yourself targets in terms of how much you want to earn. Don't aim too high but make sure that it's something you can realistically live off. Depending on the nature of your work, something like $150 a day is a good 'base rate'.

Having a target like this is a good idea because it allows you to structure everything else accordingly and to decide how much work you're going to take on and at what point in the week you're going to do it. At the same time, you can be sure that you'll be sticking to at least a minimum amount of income without going broke.

4.5 Systems

Even with a good balance of clients and no unreal expectations, you'll still likely find that things can get out of hand and you can find yourself stressed. When your client messages you at 8pm on a Friday night saying that the work you did for them isn't very good... how can you possibly ignore it? Likewise, when it turns out the software update you released to your customers had a major bug in it on Friday night... again, what can you do?

There are a few different systems and tools you can put in place that can help you in any of these situations. If you want to find more of these, then I highly recommend the book 'The Four Hour Workweek' from Tim Ferriss which goes into this sort of thing in-depth.

However, the ones supplied below should be just enough to help you significantly reduce your stress working from home so that you can start improving your health and happiness...

Auto-Responders

The first and most straightforward tool/system to use is your e-mail's auto-responder capability. This allows you to send an automated reply to your clients, customers and business partners whenever they message you after 6pm or on a weekend and this can say something like this:

"Thank you for your message. I'm afraid I will be out of the office until tomorrow at 9am and will be unable to respond until then. If you have a real emergency, then you can contact me on my home phone number at: 00 0 000000. But please don't call if it can wait until tomorrow.

My working hours are between 9am-6pm Monday-Friday."

This e-mail is perfect because it tells your clients or customers why you haven't gotten back to them and gives them a means to get in touch if they really are in a dire situation. You should find though that very few people will actually abuse your home number, so you can be safe in the knowledge that you'll be undisturbed. That said, you can also stop imagining worst-case scenarios.

Virtual Assistants

A virtual assistant is someone who can handle all types of work on your behalf as long as they don't need to be physically present. Usually these companies/individuals are based in India or in other countries with lower costs of living, so you'll likely only pay a few dollars for a day's work. Of course you get what you pay for to an extent, so don't expect amazing quality English unless you are willing to pay top dollar.

Either way though, these companies provide work that can include: booking appointments, responding to e-mails, doing research, handling marketing and SEO, proof reading, data entry and much more. You can use a digital assistant then to outsource the boring-but-time consuming aspects of your job, while you focus instead on doing what it is that you do so well. They can also stand-in for you sometimes at the weekend.

Similarly, it never hurts to know a couple of people who can help you out in a crisis. If you have a friend who works online, you can make a pact with them to bail each other out occasionally if you have too much work. You might even be able to offer some aspects of your work to friends interested in making a little extra money on the side!

Automation

There are all kinds of different tools you can use online these days to automate your work. One of the very best of these is IFTTT which essentially allows you to link different online tools and social media accounts together. For instance, IFTTT - https://ifttt.com/ (which stands for 'If This, Then That') can create a system where your Facebook posts are likewise posted to Twitter – this can save you a lot of time in a social media campaign.

But there's much more besides. You can also use this tool to copy all your Gmail contacts to a Google Drive spreadsheet, or to add Google Calendar appointments to a To Do List. IFTTT and many tools like it can act as force multipliers and save you a *lot* of time.

A Separate Phone

If you use your mobile for work, then it's highly advisable to have a *separate* mobile for your personal life. This way, you can take that phone and drop it in a drawer at the end of the day. Now you won't be disturbed by e-mails from your clients, or from customers or visitors to your website, because you won't be aware of them.

4.6 Hypothesis Testing

All these tools will do a lot to help you spend less time working and to help you 'switch off' at the end of the day. Ultimately though, you're still going to have to 'trust' in the fact that you can take time off of work or not respond immediately to an e-mail and this is the hard part.

This is also the *crucial* part though. Until you learn to *psychologically* let go of work, you're not going to get the recovery you need to be healthy and to perform optimally. Even if you aren't getting e-mails, you'll still find work takes its toll if you're lying away thinking about how to apologize to that angry e-mail.

The best way to accomplish this is with a CBT (cognitive behavioral therapy) technique called 'hypothesis testing'. Here, you think about the thing you're afraid to do and you think about what it is that is making you afraid to do it. You're afraid to ignore e-mails or turn down work because you think your clients will abandon you.

To let go of that fear then, you have to *try* not responding to e-mails sometimes. Give it a go – respond to the next e-mail you get *tomorrow* instead of right now and then just apologize for being late. In all likelihood, you'll find there are no repercussions and as a result, you'll be much more inclined to do the same thing again next time. Likewise, just *try* not updating your website for a week and see if it hurts your traffic all that much. Again, probably fine, isn't it?

4.7 Your Personal Life

Most of what we've discussed so far has revolved around designing your work to avoid it interfering with your personal life. But for this to be effective it has to work both ways and you have to make sure that your personal life isn't interfering with work. That in turn, means that you have to be strict when it comes to not taking calls, or meeting with friends during the hours of 9-5. And just as you put your work phone in a drawer in the evenings, you should consider putting your home phone in a drawer while you're working.

Of course you might decide you want to take advantage of your freedom by seeing friends more. In fact, meeting your friends on their lunch breaks can be a good way to avoid that cabin fever feeling and is always appreciated.

Or maybe you want to work in the morning and then again in the evening so you can spend the afternoon with family. Just make sure that this is pre-planned and that you have a strict cut off point for when your break ends and be consistent with that.

You can obviously give yourself the day off as well if you want to accept an exciting invitation but realize that this is a bigger commitment than it seems. You'll have to make that work up elsewhere and then it will be hard to get back into your routine. Moreover, if you bend your rules a few times, people will expect you to do it *all* the time. While it might not feel like it, being a bit strict and unsociable in the short term will actually allow you to spend *more* time with friends in the long.

Chapter 05

Optimizing Performance, Health and Productivity

———————————◆———————————

Now you have optimized your work/life balance and put systems and parameters in place to define your work hours, you should right away find that you have a lot more time and a lot more energy for working. You should be less stressed, a little less bipolar and a lot less tired.

This is the framework that will now allow you to build a truly healthy and optimal lifestyle. What you need to recognize is that your performance at work and your general health are intimately tied together. The happier and healthier you are during your time off, the better you will perform when you are working. The better you work, the more time you will have to focus on your own health.

And it all starts with sleep…

5.1 Optimizing Sleep

By employing a little strict discipline , you will find that you less often allow your work life to ruin your sleep. This is *crucial* because your output will be significantly neutered if you don't.

At the same time, you also need to make sure that you are doing everything else in your power to make sure your sleep is the best it can be.

For starters, this means going to bed at the same time every night and aiming to get a full 8 hours sleep. Again, this is *sacred* and it will make *all* the difference to every other aspect of your life. Going to bed at a strict time is what will help you set your internal rhythms, while waking up at the same time will prevent sleep inertia (and likewise prevent you from sleeping through your working morning).

Make sure that your room is *pitch dark* and that light is kept to an absolute minimum. Tape over the LEDs in the room and use heavy curtains to block out sunlight. Remember, you want to avoid 'blue light' so don't look at your phone or computer past 8pm.

Caffeine should also be avoided after 4pm and note that alcohol can *ruin* the restorative nature of your rest.

A warm shower just before bed can also make a big difference to your sleep, as can stretching and perhaps practicing a little quiet meditation (meditation is also a great tool for encouraging mental discipline so that you aren't thinking about work). Make sure you get plenty of exercise and fresh air during the day too, so that you will be more tired when it comes to the evening.

Finally, nutrition is also critical for healthy sleep and specifically you need to be consuming enough vitamin D, magnesium, zinc and tryptophan to really maximize your deep sleep.

5.2 Exercise

Exercise is also a very important tool for the self-employed. Remember, working from home means you have no commute which means less exercise. At the same time, that means you have at *least* an hour you can commit to going to the gym in the morning and this will also help to boost your brain power.

Exercise triggers the release of BDNF – brain derived neurotrophic factor – which in turn increases learning, plasticity and attention. It also helps you get more blood to your brain and improves your mood and focus. All these things are great tools for boosting your performance and for combating health complaints.

Particularly important as well is stretching. Stretching *also* boosts IQ and at the same time it can prevent the mobility issues that come from working at a computer. Yoga is a particularly good practice but you can benefit simply from doing some stretches on a mat prior to lifting weights or doing CV.

Now you might have a desire to look like Arnold Schwarzenegger in which case, you need an entirely different book. But for the purposes of optimal productivity and health, you don't need to go mad in the gym. In fact, it's better that you *don't*. Instead, focus on exercise that will be enjoyable and that you'll be likely to stick to. Your whole aim here is to *move* regularly and to apply a little bit of positive stress (eustress) to your body to wake it up and strengthen it. Bodyweight training is particularly good for this, as is running.

Ultimately, remember that it's better to have a very easy training regime that you actually stick to, than an intense one that you never do…

And in this vein, it's also pertinent to find a gym that is *near* to you, or to set up your own home gym. If the gym is 10 miles away and requires driving, then it will eat into your day *and* your available energy levels.

5.3 Nutrition

This is the most important point of all: getting your nutrition right.

Again, our goal here is not to turn you into Superman or to give you gigantic pecs. Instead, the objective is to make you generally healthy, happy and able to work well. Avoiding obesity is part of that, so you do want to cut down on your carbs. Likewise, you want to avoid carbs and sugars because they can make you tired after your blood sugar has spiked.

Instead, focus on filling up with complex carbs, fats and proteins and don't overeat. Working from home means you can eat smaller snacks instead of big meals and this is also advisable.

The most important thing to remember of all though, is that your diet should be *nutrient dense*. This means that you should focus on getting lots of fruits, lots of vegetables, lots of meats and more. The benefits that zinc, potassium, sodium, vitamin C, B complex vitamins, lutein, calcium, l-tyrosine, l-carnitine, vitamin D, iron, omega 3 fatty acid, CoQ10, MCT oils and more have on your body cannot possibly be overstated. If you are getting your RDA of all these things, you will sleep better, feel happier, be thinner, think faster, be stronger... and the effects are more profound than any 'nootropic' or 'health supplement'. The best way to do this is just to eat lots of berries, fish, fruits, leafy greens, meats, organ meats and more.

Don't cut anything out your diet and do everything you can to give your body a varied and comprehensive selection of nutrients.

5.4 Introducing Kaizen

All this might sound like a lot to take on all at once, but if you're creating a business plan that supports these changes you'll find it's much easier. The changes you make to improve your health and energy will feed into your work life and the improved work life will feed into better health and energy – it's a virtuous cycle and that's why it makes sense to change everything at once, instead of viewing your 'diet' or your 'fitness' as isolated matters.

But if it's still sounding daunting, consider the concept of kaizen. Kaizen means making a small change in your lifestyle that will have ripples affecting every other area. If you can't commit to changing your diet right away, instead just try committing to having a smoothie instead of a cappuccino first thing in the morning. Or commit to just doing 20 press ups in the evening.

This one change will likely be the beginning of huge repercussions in your life that lead to the healthy, happy, entrepreneurial you that you want to become.

Chapter 06

Home Business Models

———————◆———————

Now you know how to manage your time, your energy, your workload and your clients and you *should* be happier, healthier and more productive as a result. You're finally putting your lifestyle first and your career second and that's what working from home should really be all about.

But none of this will be much use if you don't already work from home. So if you're still working in an office and now *really* keen to start out on your own, this section is for you. What's more, this section should also show you how you can set up more side-projects, or how you can adapt your current business model into something more conducive to a healthy lifestyle.

With that in mind then, here are some basic business models to consider…

6.1 Top Home Business Models for Lifestyle Design

Services

If you want to work on a computer, there are hundreds of different services you can provide online that are in high demand these days. Popular choices include web design, programming, graphic design, photography, copywriting and marketing.

But there are others too: for instance, you can offer proof reading services, virtual assistant services, consultation, legal advice, publishing, product design, social media management and tons more. You could even become a talent agent – most jobs these days can be performed online in fact.

To start this business, all you need is to place an advert somewhere or respond to an advert. There are lots of places online that make this easy. Warrior Forum or Digital Point Forums for instance are forums frequented by website owners and digital marketers and you should be able to find lots of work here. Likewise, you can also find work by posting on outsourcing sites like Elance and UpWork. People Per Hour is another good one and you can also try simply calling or e-mailing business owners – or handing out business cards and going into stores!

This kind of work has the advantage of being straightforward – you get paid for the work you do. At the same time though, it's also a lot less scalableand it's certainly not passive. It also means you'll be *somewhat* tied to the schedule of those you're working for.

Publishing

You can make money as a website owner, blogger, YouTube vlogger or any other kind of online publisher. To do so, you just have to build the popularity of your website and add AdSense (pay per click advertising), find a sponsor or sell a product (either of your own, or for commission).

All these systems work and they're very good at bringing in passive income. The only downside is that you have to put in the work in the first place and it can take a while to start seeing returns. A good compromise stance is to try earning money form a service, while using this time to gradually build a site.

Selling Products

You can sell products for commission (called affiliate marketing), you can sell e-books from your website, you can sell an app *or* you can sell products you buy.

To do the latter, all you need to do is find a cheap way to buy items in wholesale. Find a wholesaler or look on eBay and then order your t-shirts, CDs or whatever else it is you want to sell in a bulk. If you get about 100 to start with, it won't cost you *too* much and then of course you can sell them on for more than you paid for each one individually.

You can do this through your own website again but you don't need to – just as easily, you can start selling your product through eBay or through a landing page. Once you sell off the hundred you bought, you can then reinvest the profit into 200 more and gradually grow until you're making a big turnover. Note of course that you will need somewhere to *store* the items.

Conclusion

This all sounds well and good but there's a good chance you won't go for any of these models. Why? Because you're too scared to give up your day job.

The good news for you then is that you *don't have to.* In fact, the much better way to make this work is to start with a small business and slowly grow it in your free time (as a hobby) and then to quit your job only when you have enough work.

Take two weeks off work for instance and try finding some clients to do marketing for. If you find them easily enough and they seem to be offering steady work... then you can hand in your notice.

Or start building a website on your lunch break and at weekends – it should be fun and something you enjoy anyway. If it starts making money, then you can maybe work less and eventually quit altogether.

Do bear in mind that you need to approach this plan seriously if you want it to work. If you really want to start earning a living from home, then don't come up with some elaborate plan to make the next Facebook. That might work, sure, but it's not a very reliable short term strategy for improving your lifestyle. There's no need to reinvent the wheel here – just go with a business model that has been proven to work and then execute it flawlessly.

And most of all make sure that when you do this, you also think about the lifestyle you want and *how* that business is going to help you get that lifestyle. Think about your health, think about your sleep and think about your stress levels. Is your business model designed to support the life you want, or are you still stuck in reverse?

Take Home Lessons

- Build a business plan that focusses on lifestyle first
- Remember that 'success' doesn't always lead to that lifestyle you want…
- Trial your business while you're still working and quit when it works
- There's no need to reinvent the wheel!
- Don't work in your living room, make the most of your freedom
- If you don't want to be a digital nomad, you can still take more holidays and travel in short bursts!
- Be strict and disciplined with your working hours, your social time and bed time

- Sleep is sacred!
- Eat a healthy diet full of vitamins and nutrients
- Separate your work-life and home-life by using different devices, auto responders and virtual assistants
- Make a pact with an entrepreneurial friend to help each other out in a crisis
- Try not to stress too much if you are forced to hand in work a little late
- Have multiple revenue streams

Have contingency plans Good luck!